TEEN LIFE 411

I'VE GOTTEN A DWI/DUI.

NOW WHAT?

CORONA BREZINA

ROSEN
PUBLISHING®

New York

Published in 2016 by The Rosen Publishing Group, Inc.
29 East 21st Street, New York, NY 10010

Copyright © 2016 by The Rosen Publishing Group, Inc.

First Edition

Library of Congress Cataloging-in-Publication Data

Brezina, Corona.
I've gotten a DWI/DUI. Now what?/Corona Brezina.—First edition.
        pages cm.—(Teen life 411)
Includes bibliographical references and index.
ISBN 978-1-4994-6146-6 (library bound)
1. Drunk driving—United States—Juvenile literature.
2. Drunk driving—Law and legislation—United States—Juvenile literature. 3. Teenage automobile drivers—Alcohol use—United States—Juvenile literature. I. Title.
HE5620.D72B74 2015
364.1'47—dc23

                                        2014042483

Manufactured in the United States of America

CONTENTS

You're driving home and you see the lights of a police car start flashing behind you. Your first fear is that you'll get a ticket for speeding or some other infraction. Of course, you don't look forward to explaining it to your parents or paying for the higher insurance rates. But as bad as it is to get a traffic ticket due to carelessness or bad judgment, the penalties for drinking and driving are much more severe. A driving while intoxicated or driving under the influence (DWI/DUI) charge isn't a ticketable offense—it's a misdemeanor or felony crime that involves the criminal court or juvenile justice system.

The penalties for a DWI/DUI charge are severe, and for good reason. Drunk and drugged driving are public health threats. Impaired drivers cause more than ten thousand deaths and injure hundreds of thousands more every year,

In most cases, a police officer must have probable cause for a traffic stop. A DWI/DUI offender is likely to show signs of impairment, such as swerving or erratic driving.

according to the National Highway Traffic Safety Administration (NHTSA). Public and private agencies have worked to raise awareness of the issue and take steps to reduce the harm done by drunk and drugged drivers. Some of these are prevention measures, such as screening for alcohol or drug problems during medical checkups, but most involve enforcement of the laws and sanctions for DWI/DUI offenders.

A driver convicted of a DWI/DUI will pay a large fine, have his or her license suspended or revoked, be required to attend a DUI prevention education program, see insurance rates increase if the policy isn't canceled outright, and end up with a juvenile or criminal record. Additional sanctions may be imposed depending on state law. And these are the minimum penalties for a first-time offense—the sentence is intended to deter an offender from a second offense. Punishments for subsequent offenses are much harsher.

The laws are even stricter for underage drivers. It's illegal for an adult to drive impaired, but it's illegal for a young adult under the age of twenty-one to drink alcohol in the first place and an even more serious offense to drive under the influence. A DWI/DUI is a very serious charge, and the laws pertaining to drunk driving are complex and sometimes confusing. If you're affected by a DWI/DUI case, you should acquaint yourself with the terminology, your legal rights and responsibilities, and the legal process involved in a typical DWI/DUI charge.

Even if you've never been personally involved in a DWI/DUI incident, the repercussions of drunk driving still impact you. According to the NHTSA, 10,322 people were killed in crashes involving an intoxicated driver in the United States in 2012. Hundreds of thousands more were hurt in crashes, sometimes receiving injuries that changed lives and required months or years of treatment and rehabilitation. These tragedies come with a high economic toll, as well. The NHTSA found that drunk driving cost the nation nearly $49 billion every year in property damage, insurance costs, medical bills, lost productivity, and other expenses. When factoring in the lost quality of life of the victims, the amount is quadrupled.

Reducing Alcohol-Impaired Driving

Many official reports use the term "alcohol-impaired driving" when discussing traffic safety statistics. Most people just use the less precise description "drunk driving." A driver is considered alcohol impaired if his or her blood alcohol concentration (BAC) exceeds the legal limit or if the individual's thinking and actions are affected by drugs or alcohol.

In this condition, a driver's physical coordination is diminished. Concentration and perception are affected. It might be obvious to anybody else that an alcohol-impaired individual would be a danger on the road, but alcohol impairs judgment, as well.

Drunk driving has been a problem almost since the invention of the automobile, and laws have been slow to keep pace. In 1905, for example, a wealthy twenty-two-year-old man named Barbee Hook hit and killed an elderly pedestrian while speeding through a residential area in Los Angeles, California. He had been drinking whiskey before driving. Hook was tried for manslaughter, and the case was closely followed by the press and public. The jury acquitted Hook after less than an hour of deliberation.

Throughout the first half of the twentieth century, such acquittals were common. Many state laws addressing drunk driving were lenient or inadequately enforced. After the invention of BAC testing machines, experts at the time recommended a 0.15 BAC to be the level at which an individual was considered impaired. That is nearly twice the legal limit of today. Although critics called for harsher laws and penalties for drunk driving incidents, offenders could often count on being treated lightly in court.

Drunk driving endangers the health and property of the driver, passengers, other occupants of vehicles on the road, and anyone else who happens to be in the vicinity.

In 1966, the National Highway Safety Agency was formed (today it is called the NHTSA). The agency began considering new measures related to alcohol and highway safety. Few reforms were put into place over the next fifteen years, however, and the American public showed little concern about the consequences of drunk driving.

This apathy began to change around 1980, as victims of drunk drivers turned to activism. They began publicizing their cause and putting pressure on lawmakers. In 1980, two women founded MADD— Mothers Against Drunk Drivers (later changed to Mothers Against Drunk Driving). Both women had seen their lives shattered by the actions of severely intoxicated drivers with

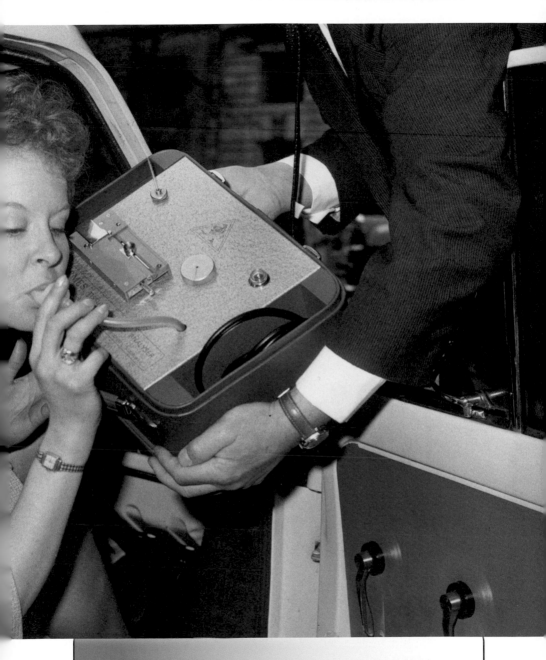

In this 1964 photograph, a woman tries out the Drink-Meter, an early version of the Breathalyzer machine that measures BAC levels.

a past history of drunk driving. Cindi Lamb's infant daughter was partially paralyzed in a car crash, and she later died from complications. Candy Lightner's teenage daughter was struck and killed by a hit-and-run drunk driver.

MADD succeeded in seizing the nation's attention and spurring genuine progress in strengthening drunk driving laws. The 1980s saw the enactment of legislation that lowered the legal BAC for drivers, toughened enforcement of laws, established the national drinking age as twenty-one, and imposed stiffer penalties for drunk drivers—especially repeat offenders. The new laws yielded results, with deaths resulting from drunk driving falling from about twenty-five thousand in 1980 to seventeen thousand in 1985, according to *Time* magazine.

In the twenty-first century, fatalities resulting from alcohol-impaired crashes have continued to decline, falling from 13,096 in 2003 to 10,322 in 2012, as reported by the NHTSA. These accounted for 31 percent of all traffic fatalities in 2012. (Different sources often report conflicting statistics, depending on terminology. For example, numbers involving alcohol-*related* rather than alcohol-*impaired* incidents will be higher. A crash is considered alcohol related if any person present at the incident had a BAC above 0.01 percent, even if the individual was, for example, a passenger in the car or a pedestrian.)

Among the 2012 fatalities, 65 percent were the alcohol-impaired drivers themselves. Sixteen percent were passengers riding with the alcohol-impaired driver. More than two hundred children were killed in alcohol-impaired driving crashes, and more than half of these were passengers in the vehicle of the alcohol-impaired driver.

In 2012, about 1.3 million people in total were arrested for driving under the influence of alcohol or drugs, according to statistics given by the Federal Bureau of Investigation (FBI). About seven thousand of these arrests were of minors under the age of eighteen, and about forty-five thousand were under the age of twenty-one. There is no typical drunk driver. An alcohol-impaired driver might be of any race or socio-economic background. NHTSA data on fatal crashes involving alcohol-impaired drivers, however, identifies some groups of people that are at higher risk for reckless driving. Men are significantly more likely than women to drive drunk. Younger drivers are more likely to drive impaired than older drivers. The highest proportion of drivers involved in fatal crashes with a BAC level of 0.08 or higher were ages twenty-one to twenty-four, followed by ages twenty-five to thirty-four, and then thirty-five to forty-four. Repeat offenders—drivers with a prior conviction—were disproportionately more likely to drive with a BAC level of 0.08 or higher.

UNDERAGE AND DANGEROUS

In 2012, about 750 drivers under the age of twenty-one—the legal drinking age—were found to have a BAC of 0.08

DRUGGED DRIVING

Most DWI/DUI offenses involve alcohol-impaired driving, but drugged driving is also a serious problem on the roads. According to a 2012 National Institute on Drug Abuse (NIDA) survey, 10.3 million people admitted to having driven under the influence of illicit drugs during the previous year, compared to 29.1 million people who admitted driving while under the influence of alcohol. Many drivers involved in accidents have both drugs and alcohol in their systems. Drugs that cause impaired driving include illicit drugs as well as legal prescription drugs.

Drugged driving is more problematic for police to enforce and for prosecutors to prove in court. Different drugs each produce different impairing effects that are more complex and unpredictable than those of alcohol. A 2009 NHTSA report admitted that "current knowledge about the effects of drugs other than alcohol is insufficient to allow the identification of dosage limits that are related to elevated crash risk." Blood tests don't necessarily reflect impairment, and there are not yet any national standards for screening. The field sobriety tests for alcohol impairment do not always detect drugged drivers. Nevertheless, the federal government takes the issue seriously and has recommended that states adopt stricter laws addressing drugged driving.

or higher after being involved in a fatal crash, according to the NHTSA. (By contrast, fewer than 350 drivers over the age of sixty-five had a BAC over 0.08.) Motor vehicle crashes are the leading cause of death for teenagers, making up over one-third of all deaths. In 2012, about a quarter of all young drivers killed in accidents had a BAC of 0.08 or higher.

Drunk driving can lead to tragic consequences, and at all BAC levels, teenage drivers are at greater risk of being involved in a crash than older adults.

Young drivers, drunk or sober, are more likely to be involved in crashes than the general population. Although only 6 percent of all licensed drivers are under the age of twenty, 9 percent of all fatal crashes and 13 percent of all police-reported crashes involved young drivers. Young drivers are simply more inexperienced and more likely to make driving errors. Nonetheless, teens tend to be over-confident regarding their own driving skills.

Teenagers are also more likely than older drivers to take risks and act impulsively. Crashes involving young drivers are often due to speeding. Teenagers are less likely to wear seat belts, especially when they've been drinking. They're more likely to drive distracted, such as by texting while driving. Having passengers in the car with a young driver increases the chances of risk taking by the driver, in addition to serving as yet another distraction. Teenagers are also more likely than adults to binge drink—consuming many drinks at one sitting—which puts them at a higher risk for impaired driving.

UNDER THE INFLUENCE

No matter why people choose to drink, the result is the same: they're physically and mentally affected by the alcohol. After drinking a small amount of alcohol,

Alcohol significantly affects a drinker's physical and mental state. Someone who has been drinking may exhibit drastic mood swings and aggressive behavior.

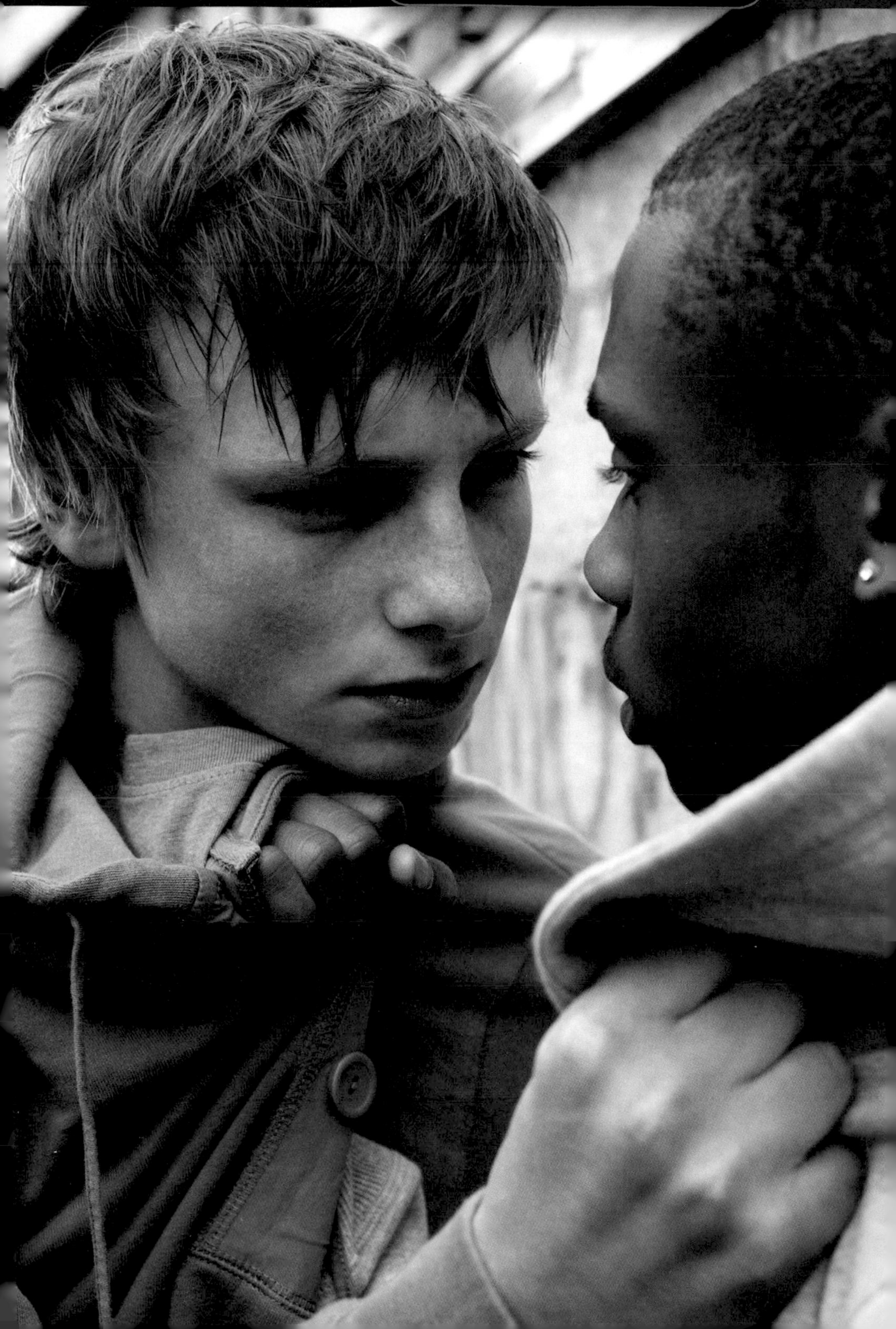

Alcohol impairs a driver's judgment, concentration, comprehension of surroundings, coordination, reaction time, and even the ability to see and hear clearly.

people begin to feel relaxed. After one or two drinks, alcohol begins to have physical effects, in addition to more conspicuous effects on thinking and behavior. Even though an individual's BAC level is still under the legal driving limit at this point, a person's coordination, judgment, and other faculties are already diminished.

At 0.08 BAC, when a person is considered alcohol impaired under the law, he or she is in no condition—mentally or physically—to drive. Muscle coordination is reduced—causing problems with balance, vision, reaction time, and hearing. Mental capabilities are also diminished—leading

to reduced capacity concerning judgment, self-control, reasoning, and memory. At high levels of impairment—such as at 0.15 BAC, nearly twice the legal limit—a person will likely appear highly uncoordinated and confused. Extremely high BAC levels, between 0.30 and 0.40 BAC, can lead to coma and death.

The effects of alcohol impair driving ability from the moment a driver exercises bad judgment and gets behind the wheel. Impaired drivers have difficulty judging distances and determining the direction of sound. They lack the coordination to steer, accelerate, and use the brakes, which could easily lead to a crash going around a curve. Because of a reduced ability to concentrate, they're likely to have trouble paying attention to more than one task at a time, such as staying in the lane, visually tracking other vehicles, and holding a conversation with passengers. If an emergency situation arises, an alcohol-impaired driver probably won't be able to react quickly.

The amount of alcohol necessary to reach 0.08 BAC varies from one person to another. An individual's weight is a factor—a larger person will require more alcohol to become impaired. Men generally metabolize alcohol faster than women, meaning that a woman will require less alcohol to reach 0.08 BAC than a man of the same weight. Other factors that affect a person's reaction to alcohol include age, race, amount of food eaten beforehand, pace of drinking, and any use of drugs or medications. One's past history of alcohol use can also affect how fast alcohol is metabolized—habitual drinkers metabolize alcohol more quickly.

Therefore, someone who has "just had two or three drinks" could either be negligibly affected or alcohol impaired. A BAC test can measure the precise amount of alcohol in a person's system. BAC expresses the ratio of alcohol in the blood as a percentage. Someone with a BAC of 0.08 has eight parts alcohol for every ten thousand parts blood.

BAC levels can be determined by a blood test, breath test, or urine test. The blood test is the most accurate, the urine test the least. If you want to estimate how many drinks it would take for you to reach a certain BAC, there are charts and calculators on the Internet that will give you an approximation based on your weight, gender, number of drinks, and length of time in which they were consumed.

CHAPTER 2

KNOW THE LAW

Specific laws concerning drunk driving vary widely from one state to another. In most states, an individual arrested for drunk or drugged driving is charged with driving under the influence, or DUI. A handful of states use an alternative acronym, DWI, which can signify either driving while intoxicated or driving while impaired. In some of these states, a DUI qualifies as a separate offense from a DWI. It may be either a more severe charge (such as in Maryland) or a lesser charge (such as in Texas). Some states also consider the offense of operating, rather than driving, a vehicle while impaired. These charges— OUI or OWI—are broader than DWI/DUI. An intoxicated person who is asleep in a parked car with the ignition switched off may be considered to be in control of the vehicle under the law and can be charged with an OUI.

Someone who has been drinking shouldn't get behind the wheel for any reason. In some states, being caught drunk even in a stationary vehicle can have legal consequences.

DWI/DUI
OFFENSES

Someone arrested for a DWI/DUI often faces two charges for the same offense. The first is for driving under the influence, which is demonstrated if the driver exhibits signs of impairment during the incident. A witness might state that he or she saw the driver swerving or driving erratically, or the police might administer field sobriety tests. State laws on impairment vary—one state might require an "appreciable impairment" for a DWI/DUI charge, while another requires only the "slightest degree" of impairment. State laws also vary depending on the scenario. Some states require that a driver be operating a vehicle on a

A woman caused a boat collision on a lake in New Hampshire, allegedly while drunk, that killed her best friend. She served six months in prison for negligent homicide and six months of electronic home confinement. She also lost her privilege to operate a boat for three years.

public road to be charged with a DWI/DUI. States also differ on what is considered a motor vehicle. People have been charged with DWI/DUI while using golf carts, bicycles, lawn mowers, mopeds, and snowmobiles. There is also an analogous boating under the influence (BUI) charge, with similar penalties as those for a DWI/DUI.

The other charge is DWI/DUI per se, which is based solely on BAC. If a breath test yields a BAC of 0.08 or over, no further proof of impairment is necessary for a DWI/DUI per se charge. Most DWI/DUI cases involve alcohol impairment, but about eighteen states also have per se laws that address drug impairment. A blood test must yield a positive result for the presence of a prohibited substance in a person's system for a DWI/DUI per se charge involving drugs. Most states with these laws have a zero tolerance policy for illicit drugs.

During a routine traffic stop, an officer checks on a driver's driving privilege status—which reveals whether a license is suspended or revoked—and record of previous traffic convictions.

IGNITION INTERLOCK

An ignition interlock is a device similar to a Breathalyzer that is connected to a vehicle's dashboard. The driver must provide a breath sample before starting the ignition. If the device detects a BAC above a certain limit, the engine won't start. The device records data such as vehicle use, alcohol use, and attempts to tamper with the ignition interlock. Violations may lead to increased sanctions for the offender.

Every state in the United States has passed laws requiring or allowing the use of ignition interlocks as a penalty for DWI/DUI offenders, mandated either by the Department of Motor Vehicles (DMV) or the courts. The device has proven to be an effective means of preventing drivers from committing subsequent DWI/DUI offenses.

Ignition interlock devices can keep the roads safer by requiring that DWI/DUI offenders prove that they are sober before operating a vehicle.

Someone can be charged with a DWI/DUI even if BAC is under 0.08 if a police officer observes evidence of impairment. Experts agree that alcohol can have a significant effect at lower BAC levels. If an individual drives recklessly or fails sobriety tests, he or she may be charged with driving under the influence even with a BAC between 0.05 and 0.08. Some states consider this offense as driving while ability impaired (DWAI), a slightly lesser charge than a DWI/DUI.

A DWI/DUI case can be charged as either a misdemeanor or a felony, which is a much more serious offense. A first-time DWI/DUI is generally charged as a misdemeanor, but it can qualify as a felony if somebody was injured in the incident. Repeat offenses are also charged as felonies in some states.

Regardless of the particulars of state laws, anyone convicted of a drunk or drugged driving offense will be listed on the National Driver Register (NDR), a database of problem drivers. Drivers who have had their license suspended or revoked for any reason will be listed in the register, in addition to offenders convicted of serious traffic violations such as a DWI/DUI. State and federal driver licensing agencies have access to the information on the NDR. This means that if you move from one state to another, you'd better address a driver's license suspension before applying for a license in the new state. It also means that administrators processing information about a DWI/DUI will be aware of convictions in other states. A few other federal agencies, such as the National

Alcohol-impaired drivers are likely to fail field or roadside sobriety tests, which are commonly used by police to establish probable cause for a DWI/DUI arrest.

Transportation Safety Board (NTSB), also have access to the NDR. You can check to see if you have a record by making an official request to the NDR.

A DWI/DUI ARREST

A police officer must have probable cause to make a DWI/DUI arrest, meaning that the suspect's behavior must suggest he or she is under the influence. A driver may drift out of the lane, brake too early or too late, or have trouble maintaining a constant speed. He or she might make bad judgment calls, such as following another vehicle too closely, or have problems with vigilance, such as failing to obey traffic signals. A police officer might stop an individual for an unrelated violation, such as a broken taillight.

Once the driver is pulled over, an officer may observe further cues that the driver is intoxicated, such as fumbling or slurred speech. A driver may give incriminating statements, such as admitting to drinking or using drugs. A police officer can legally search the car if he or she has probable cause to believe that the driver might be holding drugs. If a police officer is called to the scene of an accident, he or she will watch for indications that anyone involved is under the influence.

Police also assess whether a driver is intoxicated by conducting field sobriety tests. There are three standardized sobriety tests. For the horizontal gaze nystagmus (HGN) test, a driver follows a moving object such as a pen or flashlight with his or her eyes. A jerking of the eyes and an inability to track the object indicates impairment. For the walk-and-turn test, a driver follows the officer's instructions to take nine straight steps heel-to-toe, turn on one foot, and follow the same path back. For the one-leg-stand test, a driver stands on one foot and counts the seconds aloud. The walk-and-turn test and the one-leg-stand test assess coordination as well as whether a driver can divide his or attention between two simple tasks at once, such as listening to instructions while moving. In some states, field sobriety tests are voluntary and a driver can refuse to consent. However, a police officer may interpret a refusal as evidence of guilt.

A police officer may also administer a preliminary alcohol screening (PAS) as a component of the field sobriety tests. This is a different process from the mandatory chemical test, which is given later. The PAS measures an individual's BAC using a breath-testing machine that yields an instantaneous result. As with other field tests, the PAS is voluntary. If impairment by drugs is suspected, the police might call in a certified drug recognition expert (DRE) to examine the driver.

After the field tests and PAS, the police administer a mandatory chemical test that is required by implied consent laws. This means that when you applied for your driver's license, you agreed to submit to the test if suspected of a DWI/DUI. The police may offer a choice of what type of test—either blood or breath for alcohol (a urine test is also a possibility, but it is less accurate and many states have discontinued it) or a blood or urine test for drugs.

The consequences for refusing to take the mandatory chemical test are severe. Depending on state laws, the driver may lose his or his license for up to eighteen months and have sanctions added to the license. He or she may have to pay a fine or comply with an ignition interlock requirement. The refusal to take the test can itself be used as evidence in court that the driver was probably impaired, and it may ultimately lead to stiffer penalties if convicted. And even if the driver is exonerated in court, he or she is still held accountable for refusing to take the mandatory test.

The police can legally take a blood draw by force. Usually this is done only in extreme circumstances, such as when someone is killed.

After a driver is arrested for a DWI/DUI, he or she will probably be booked at the police station, during which the information on the crime is formally processed. The offender's car may be towed and taken to an impound lot. Typically, the offender will be detained in jail—probably in the so-called drunk tank—and then either be released on his or her own recognizance or else be required to meet bail before being freed.

YOUNG AND IMPAIRED

A teenager pulled over for a DWI/DUI will undergo the same process as an adult. A parent or guardian will be contacted if a minor is taken into custody, however, and the juvenile court system will conduct the formal proceedings.

The laws concerning DWI/DUI are even tougher for underage drivers than for adults. Because the legal drinking age is twenty-one in every state, young adults who drink are already breaking the law before getting behind the wheel. This is an example of a status offense, an action that is illegal for minors but not considered a crime for adults.

State laws for underage drinking and driving are correspondingly more stringent for young drivers. In general, anyone under the age of twenty-one can be charged with a DWI/DUI if his or her BAC is 0.02 or higher. Some states are even stricter, setting the limit at 0.01 BAC, or zero tolerance for any alcohol level. A state may have different levels of penalties depending on the BAC of a young driver, such as a lighter sentence if the BAC is 0.02 or below, a stiffer sentence for a BAC between 0.02 and 0.08, and the greatest penalties for a BAC above 0.08.

A DWI/DUI arrest of a minor or underage driver may be accompanied by charges for related status offenses involving alcohol. The offender may also be charged with consumption of alcohol by a minor or possession of alcohol by a minor. The use of a fake ID to buy alcohol adds another charge. If any underage passengers in the car have also been drinking, the driver may face a charge of supplying alcohol to minors.

MYTH

I won't get drunk if I'm only drinking beer.

FACT

The amount of alcohol, not the type of drink, affects whether a person becomes intoxicated. A 12-ounce (0.35-liter) beer, a 5-ounce (0.15-l) glass of wine, or a 1.5-ounce (0.04-l) shot of liquor—standard sizes for each drink—all contain about the same amount of alcohol.

MYTH

A person drinking alcohol can sober up enough to drive if he or she drinks some coffee or takes a cold shower.

FACT

There's no shortcut that can speed up the metabolism of alcohol in the body. Taking a nap or going for a walk won't do it either. These tricks may make a person more alert, but mental and physical functioning are still impaired.

MYTH

If a driver's BAC is under 0.08, he or she can't be charged with a DWI/DUI.

FACT

If the police determine that a driver is impaired by alcohol or drugs—such as by administering field sobriety tests— he or she can be arrested for a DWI/DUI. If the driver's BAC is over 0.08, he or she faces an additional charge of DWI/DUI per se.

CHAPTER 3

FACING A
DWI/DUI CHARGE

After a DWI/DUI arrest, an accused offender becomes a defendant in a court case. The process can end after just a couple appearances and a guilty plea, or it can drag out through a trial. It ends with either an acquittal or a conviction, in which case the offender receives a penalty from the judge.

DWI/DUI cases are a contentious and highly emotional topic. Many people are incensed by the thought of drunk drivers trying to avoid taking responsibility for the consequences of their actions. In general, the law has followed this trend. Every state in the nation has adopted the 0.08 BAC standard for drunk driving offenses, with the final few states passing legislation in the mid-2000s. Many states have also passed requirements that DWI/DUI offenders have an ignition interlock installed in their vehicles.

Nonetheless, defendants in criminal trials are presumed innocent until proven guilty. DWI/DUI defendants, as well as their victims, have the right to receive justice through the workings of the legal system.

UNDERSTANDING THE SYSTEM

Before an arrested DWI/DUI offender is released, he or she receives a date for a court appearance. An offender between the ages of eighteen and twenty-one will be tried in adult criminal court. Minors under the age of eighteen will generally be dealt with in juvenile court. Young offenders are sometimes tried as adults in criminal court, but this generally occurs in cases involving very serious crimes, such as a felony DWI/DUI in which someone was severely injured or killed.

The procedures and objectives of the juvenile justice system differ from those of the adult criminal justice system. To start with, juvenile court has its own terminology. From the very start, an offender is not said to be "arrested;" he or she is "taken into custody" and proceeds to the "intake department," rather than being "booked." Instead of a "sentence," a young offender receives a "disposition." An adult criminal may be "found guilty," while a juvenile offender is "adjudicated delinquent."

Proceedings in juvenile court tend to be less formal than those of adult criminal court. Early on in the process, minor offenders may be given the option of diversion rather than formal court hearings. If they accept, they admit guilt to the charges but do not establish a juvenile court record. They must complete the diversion requirements, which might include counseling, community service, restitution, and informal probation.

A juvenile adjudication hearing is similar in many ways to a criminal trial. The prosecution and defense make their cases before a judge (the juvenile justice system does not have trial by jury). They call witnesses

A DWI/DUI arrest triggers involvement in the juvenile or adult court system that continues from the arraignment through completion of the sentence.

and offer evidence. The juvenile justice system, however, focuses on rehabilitation to a greater extent than the adult criminal justice system, which concentrates more on punishment of the offender. When a young offender is adjudicated delinquent, the judge decides on a disposition that upholds public safety and holds the offender accountable but that also takes into account the offender's social history, such as family circumstances and juvenile record. The judge considers the specific needs of the offender. A disposition commonly includes treatment and rehabilitation components.

A DAY IN COURT

Offenders over the age of eighteen begin the process of a criminal court case. Soon after the arrest, the offender must attend an arraignment, the court appearance in which the judge reads the charges against the defendant to those assembled in the court and asks for a plea. The options in most states are guilty, not

SOBRIETY CHECKPOINTS: TWO VIEWS

Sobriety checkpoints are temporary roadblocks set up to stop drivers at random—every five cars, for example—where police check for alcohol or drug impairment. Checkpoints are generally conducted over weekends or holidays, late at night, when drivers are more likely to be impaired. The public is notified in advance that there will be a checkpoint, but the exact location is not announced. The mere existence of the checkpoints is intended to prevent DWI/DUIs.

Opponents of sobriety checkpoints argue that they infringe on constitutional rights, such as the requirement that the police have probable cause for a search. The practice is prohibited in eleven states. The Supreme Court, however, ruled that the public interest in curbing impaired driving outweighs the intrusion. Critics also claim that other police techniques are more effective in catching drunk drivers. Saturation patrols, for example, target erratic drivers within a certain geographic area known for high rates of alcohol-impaired driving.

guilty, or no contest, also known as nolo contendere. A no-contest plea means that the defendant accepts the punishment for the crime but does not claim innocence or admit guilt.

A guilty plea or a no-contest plea both lead to immediate conviction. The defendant signs forms disclosing the possible penalties for the crime. The case does not go to trial.

A defendant may plead not guilty and try to plea bargain at some point before the trial. In a plea agreement, the defendant agrees to plead guilty if the prosecution grants concessions that generally lighten the punishment for the crime. The prosecutor may reduce the charge— for example, California allows a defendant in a DUI case to plea bargain for a lesser charge called a wet reckless. A lawyer representing an offender with a clean driving record and a BAC that is not significantly over 0.08 will possibly be able to have the DUI charge reduced to wet reckless, which carries lesser penalties. Other plea bargain options include dropping one of the charges if the defendant pleads guilty to the other or offering deals such as a smaller fine or an agreement to perform community service.

Plea agreements are not always an option for DWI/DUI defendants. A DWI/DUI is a serious charge, and a plea bargain can appear to send the message that the prosecutor is letting the offender get off easy. Some states do not even permit plea agreements in DWI/DUI cases. And even if a prosecutor does negotiate a plea agreement with the defense, the judge may refuse to approve it.

The next court appearance before the trial is generally the preliminary hearing, in which the judge hears evidence and decides whether the prosecution has enough evidence to make a convincing case in the courtroom. If not, the judge may dismiss the case. The defense may also make pretrial motions, such as arguments that

During a DWI/DUI trial, a judge and often a jury evaluate the evidence presented by the prosecution and defense and find the defendant guilty or not guilty.

the case should be thrown out or that certain evidence should be suppressed.

If a DWI/DUI case does reach a trial, it may be heard either by a judge or, more often, by a jury. The proceedings begin with jury selection and then continue with opening statements, witness testimony and cross-examination by both sides, closing arguments, the judge's instruction to the jury, jury deliberation, and the jury verdict. Throughout, the prosecution makes arguments for a conviction and the defense tries to demonstrate that the prosecution falls short of proving guilt. A defense lawyer may try to cast doubt on evidence, such as by questioning the

accuracy of a urine test for BAC. He or she may challenge whether a police officer had valid probable cause to make an arrest. The defense attorney may also offer an alternative explanation for evidence of intoxication, such as by claiming that apparent impairment was due to a medical condition, or the attorney may introduce new evidence, such as witness testimony that the defendant had not been drinking heavily before driving.

In addition to criminal court, offenders may have to deal with sanctions imposed by the DMV or other state transit agency related to the DWI/DUI. A driver's license is typically suspended or revoked following a DWI/DUI arrest. If an offender wants to make a case for revoking the suspension, he or she can request an administrative review hearing. The hearing is separate from the proceedings in criminal court, and it does not establish guilt or innocence. It gives the offender a chance to show that the suspension was unjustified, such as by proving that the police officer did not have probable cause or that BAC was not over 0.08. Even if the DMV does agree to revoke or reduce the sanctions, the criminal court also has separate authority to suspend or revoke a license. The offender could lose driving privileges once again if found guilty of the DWI/DUI in court.

AGGRAVATED DWI/DUI

The irresponsible choices and actions of impaired drivers can lead to serious consequences for the safety of the people around them. A DWI/DUI may be accompanied by additional charges related to the incident, or it may qualify as a more serious category of offense. A first-time offense in which nobody is injured is considered a misdemeanor. Other categories of alcohol- and drug-related violations may qualify as felonies. Aggravating factors—circumstances that make the crime more severe—can lead to "enhanced," or harsher penalties. In addition, laws vary from one state to another. On every level, having a prior conviction on one's record will trigger tougher punishments for a repeat offense.

An underage driver can be charged with a DWI/DUI for having any BAC above the state's minimum, which may be 0.02 or less. If the underage driver has a BAC above 0.08, he or she may be charged for regular DWI/DUI offenses as well as the underage charge.

As stated earlier, refusing to take a mandatory BAC test is a separate offense with consequences separate from the DWI/DUI charge. A driver who refuses has his or her license suspended for a much longer period than for the DWI/DUI—with almost no chance of winning it back in the administrative review hearing—in addition to other penalties.

If an intoxicated driver is found driving with an open container of alcohol within reach in the car, the driver will be charged with violating the open-container laws that are enforced in many states. On its own, an open-container violation is generally a ticketable offense. As evidence in a DWI/DUI case, it could lead to a harsher punishment.

Driving without a valid driver's license is in itself an offense that carries significant penalties, including a fine,

If a DWI/DUI offender causes a crash that leads to someone being seriously injured or killed, it is a serious offense that qualifies as a felony.

lengthy further suspension of the license, and the possibility of time in jail. (This crime refers to driving while one's license is suspended or revoked, not merely because of leaving it at home inadvertently.) When the charge of driving without a license is added to the DWI/DUI charge, the penalty will be severe—costly fines, time in prison, and a license suspension lasting years is likely.

Some states treat impaired driving charges differently depending on whether they involves alcohol or drugs, categorizing driving under the influence of drugs (DUID) as a separate offense. There may also be enhanced penalties for an extremely high

BAC, one that is two or three times the legal limit. This charge is sometimes referred to as aggravated DWI/DUI or extreme DWI/DUI.

Reckless driving or extreme speeding when added to a DWI/DUI leads to harsher penalties. Another aggravating factor is the presence of minors in the vehicle, which may be considered child endangerment. Driving impaired in a school zone may also trigger enhanced penalties.

The most serious charges related to DWI/DUI involve crashes, especially when a victim is injured or killed. A DWI/DUI can be combined with a hit-and-run charge if the offender flees the scene. If someone was hurt in a crash that involved a DWI/DUI, the offender may be charged with serious bodily injury. If someone was killed in the crash, the offender could be charged with manslaughter, vehicular or reckless homicide, or murder in the third or second degree.

DO YOU NEED A LAWYER?

It is crucial that a defendant in a criminal or juvenile justice court case understand his or her legal rights. Court proceedings are detailed and complex. An attorney who specializes in DWI/DUI cases knows the relevant laws and procedures. He or she will be aware of the technical aspects involved in every step of the court process. The main advantage to hiring an attorney is the chance that his or her expertise may

A DWI/DUI offense is subject to harsher penalties if it occurs in a school zone, which generally qualifies as the area within a 1,000-foot (305-meter) range of school property.

A victim injured in a crash caused by a DWI/DUI offender may have the right to be compensated for medical bills, property damage, and other expenses. A DWI/DUI offender should seek legal counsel to assist in navigating the case and any injury claims.

lead to a lighter sentence. In addition, an attorney will help the defendant deal with routine administrative details and unanticipated consequences of a DUI, from filing insurance forms to registering for an alcohol treatment program. Young offenders also have the legal right to counsel and stand to gain the same benefits as adult offenders.

In some circumstances, however, hiring a lawyer may not have much impact on the outcome of the case. For a first-time offense in which there is no question of guilt, with no aggravating factors, a judge is likely to hand down a standard penalty. If a defendant

immediately pleads guilty and is convicted, legal representation probably will not change the sentence.

A defendant would be well advised to hire a lawyer for more complex or serious charges. A lawyer may be able to identify uncertainties in the prosecution's case that could lead to reduced charges or a less severe punishment. Lawyers will know whether plea bargaining is likely to be feasible. If a defendant wants to plead no contest rather than guilty, a lawyer will be familiar with the relevant laws. A DWI/DUI defendant with a case going to trial is definitely better off being represented by an attorney rather than attempting to navigate court proceedings alone. Defendants facing repeat or aggravated charges, which carry severe penalties, should seek legal counsel.

Low-income defendants may qualify for a court-appointed attorney. Public defenders are qualified lawyers who know their way around the local court system, but they often maintain a large caseload and lack resources, especially to devote to a single case.

DWI/DUI convictions carry stiff sentences that usually go beyond a fine. One of the first questions asked by offenders is, "Will I have to go to jail?" In some cases, even a conviction for a first offense may lead to mandatory jail time, as well as various other penalties and requirements. Subsequent offenses and more serious offenses receive harsher punishments. Penalties for drugged driving offenses tend to vary more from state to state than penalties for alcohol-related offenses.

A DWI/DUI offender can't change the fact that the drunk or drugged driving incident happened, but some common-sense measures can prevent the consequences from being even worse than the standard penalties. An offender shouldn't miss a court date. He or she should take care to avoid social situations that might involve drugs or alcohol and should abide by any restrictions during the court process, especially the driver's license suspension. Some lawyers advise that their clients take initiative and enroll in substance abuse programs before being ordered to do so by the court. This proves that they are sincere in addressing their problems with drugs or alcohol.

A DWI/DUI offender will be forced to find alternative transportation options to driving during the period of driver's license suspension.

DRIVING RESTRICTIONS

A DWI/DUI charge is almost certain to lead to some loss of driving privileges. Most states allow a police officer to confiscate the license of a drunk driver during the arrest if he or she has a BAC of 0.08 or higher. This triggers an administrative license suspension by the DMV. The officer usually issues a temporary license that is valid for a month, though the length varies from one state to another. The offender can challenge the suspension during this period. If the license is not reinstated, the administrative suspension begins once the temporary license expires. A three-month suspension is typical for a first offense.

A conviction in court can include a separate license suspension or revocation as part of the sentence. A court-imposed suspension for a first-time offender may last up to a year. State laws vary greatly—some states require a year's suspension, while in others the suspension period can last less than a month.

Underage offenders face similar license suspension and revocation penalties as adults. Because a BAC of 0.02 qualifies as a DWI/DUI for drivers under twenty-one, underage offenders face comparable punishments for a slighter offense. Young offenders who are dealt with in juvenile court may be sentenced under a different set of guidelines. For example, in Ohio, a nineteen-year-old with a BAC above 0.02 will generally be charged with operating a vehicle after underage consumption (OVUAC), which carries a penalty of a license suspension for up to two years. If his or her BAC is above 0.08, it results in an operating a vehicle under the influence charge (OVI, equivalent to a DUI), which triggers an administrative license suspension as well as a potential court-ordered license suspension of up to three years. An OVUAC dealt with in juvenile court may also result in a possible two-year suspension.

Many states require DWI/DUI offenders to have an ignition interlock device installed in their cars for a certain period of time once they've regained driving privileges. The devices are not always mandated for first-time offenders, but some states offer the option of shortening the length of a driver's license suspension or revocation if the offender agrees to install the device.

DWI/DUI offenders may be able to obtain a restricted or hardship license during the period in which their license is suspended. This will grant them the right to drive to work, medical appointments, and other essential trips, often only during certain hours. Installation of an ignition interlock device may be required. Restricted licenses can be especially important for people living in rural areas with no public transportation. Underage drivers are less likely to be granted a restricted license, but they may qualify if they need to drive to school or work. Some states require a waiting period before restricted driving privileges can be reinstated.

Laws may affect a driver's vehicle, as well. The police often have an offender's car towed after the arrest. Sometimes the driver must wait twelve hours before being allowed to retrieve it from the impoundment lot, a restriction intended to prevent the driver from trying to reclaim it while still drunk. A few states require that a DWI/DUI conviction be indicated on an offender's plates, such as by a certain series of numbers or letters, by the plate's color, or by a sticker.

The laws concerning driving restrictions are often much more severe for repeat offenders and those who commit more serious offenses. License suspension and revocation periods are longer. In some states, for an offender who has been convicted five times, the revocation is permanent. The ignition interlock device is more likely to be mandatory and required for a longer period. Vehicles may be impounded or confiscated for a greater length of time.

DWI/DUI offenders often add up the costs of their crime during DUI education programs, which are generally required as part of their sentences. A first-time DWI/DUI offense with no aggravating circumstances can cost a driver more than $10,000. The fine—typically around $500 but potentially more than $1,000—is just the beginning. Hiring a lawyer experienced in DWI/DUI cases can cost $5,000 or more. And you have to pay for every phase of the process, including a towing fee ($215), bail ($150–$2,000), court costs ($800), alcohol evaluation ($150), DUI education program ($250), ignition interlock device installation ($100), and license reinstatement ($125). On top of that, ongoing expenses include the interlock ignition device rental ($60 per month) and increased insurance premiums (rates tripled). These are rough estimates—actual costs vary depending on the state and specific circumstances of the case, and there will probably be many more miscellaneous fees. In addition, the court process can lead to missed time at work or even job loss, costing you income. You'll also have to pay for alternative transportation if your driver's license is suspended. Regardless of the exact total, a DWI/DUI is definitely the most expensive car trip of your life

THE HIGH COST OF A DWI/DUI

Because a DWI/DUI offender won't be driving away a vehicle after the arrest, he or she may have to pay for towing, as well as related expenses such as impoundment fees.

Some states allow for offenders' vehicles to be immobilized, such as with a wheel-locking device, or even seized and forfeited in extreme circumstances, meaning that the vehicle is auctioned off. Other possible penalties include having license plates seized or the vehicle registration revoked.

PAYING THE PRICE AND DOING TIME

A DWI/DUI penalty will include a fine. A first-time offender can expect to pay a minimum of a few hundred dollars and up to several thousand dollars, depending on state law. In addition, various court and administrative fees are charged for towing, license reinstatement, ignition interlock device upkeep, and other miscellaneous expenses. Underage offenders and juvenile offenders are also subject to fines and fees. In Ohio, for example, the charge of OVUAC for drivers under the age of twenty-one results in a fine of up to $250, and a full OVI carries a fine that ranges from $375 to more than $1,000. The fines for subsequent offenses are much greater, and in some states an offender who has been convicted three or more times can face fines of tens of thousands of dollars.

A first DWI/DUI offense carries the possibility of jail time, even without any aggravating circumstances. By definition, a misdemeanor is punishable by up to a year

A first-time DWI/DUI offense generally doesn't result in a jail sentence, but aggravating factors could lead to the offender being locked up.

DWI/DUI sentences for juveniles generally include completion of rehabilitation requirements, such as counseling, therapy, or participation in self-help programs.

in jail. Some states do mandate a short minimum sentence, such as twenty-four hours, forty-eight hours, or a few days. However, a state may allow community service to be substituted for some or all of the minimum sentence time. The maximum penalty—whether it's ninety days, six months, or longer—is usually not imposed for a first offense.

Serious and repeat DWI/DUI offenders will receive much lengthier sentences. A second conviction, which in many states is calculated within a span of ten years from the first arrest, may receive sanctions at least twice as severe as the first. Mandatory minimum sentences are longer, and some states require even lengthier sentences for offenders whose second offense occurs within a year or two of the first. A third or fourth offense may qualify as a felony, as do serious offenses that lead to injury or death. A felony conviction carries a longer sentence in prison, rather than a shorter stretch in jail.

Some DWI/DUI offenders may be given the option of house arrest rather than jail or prison time. They must wear electronic monitoring ankle bracelets and may also be required to submit to Breathalyzer tests

Before having driving privileges reinstated, a DWI/DUI offender must have proof submitted that he or she has completed all of the terms of the sentence.

on machines in their homes multiple times each day to prove that they haven't been drinking.

DWI/DUI sentences for young offenders in the juvenile justice system vary greatly depending on state law and even on local court practices. Some courts tend to view juvenile detention as harmful for juvenile offenders and focus more on treatment, especially for first-time offenders. Other courts may be more likely to require time in juvenile detention. As with adult offenders, repeat offenders and those who commit serious offenses are likelier to be punished with longer sentences, as are offenders who are transferred to adult court due to the severity of their crimes.

ADDITIONAL REQUIREMENTS

The penalties for a DWI/DUI go beyond punishment measures for the offense, such as fines and jail time. Prevention measures aim to keep the offender from committing the crime again. Examples include driver's license suspension and the ignition interlock device.

Another important objective in sentencing DWI/DUI offenders is rehabilitation, which involves measures intended to change the offender's behavior. A DWI/

DUI offender is often required to complete education or treatment programs for alcohol or drugs. Completion is often a condition for having driving privileges reinstated. Juvenile offenders are especially likely to be handed down penalties that include education, treatment, and counseling components.

In many states, an offender must undergo an evaluation or assessment interview about drug and alcohol use before sentencing. The process is conducted by a treatment agency approved by the state. The offender must submit documents such as the police report of the DWI/DUI arrest, a record of the BAC at the time of the arrest, and driving history. The assessment may include a test gauging the driver's level of risk and an interview. The results of the assessment determine an appropriate level of treatment for alcohol or drug abuse.

A common requirement is completion of DUI education programs, sometimes called risk education or risk reduction classes. States generally designate offenders to certain programs after the assessment, according to the level of the offenders' risk. Drivers considered to be at a lower risk—usually first-time offenders without an extremely high BAC—are sentenced to shorter programs than those who commit more serious offenses.

An offender assessed to be at a low risk, such as an underage first-time offender with a low BAC at the time of arrest, might complete the DUI education requirements by attending twelve hours of alcohol education classes. The course will address the effects of drugs or alcohol, the consequences of abuse and addiction, and preventing future DWI/DUIs. Attendance, participation, and behavior in class are all evaluated. At the end, the program provides the court and DMV with a certificate stating that the offender has completed the course.

Offenders at higher levels of risk are required to complete longer-term treatment programs. A standard course for a first-time DWI/DUI offender might include thirty hours over a period of three months. Offenders are required to attend alcohol education classes and may also receive counseling or participate in drug abuse treatment. High-risk offenders with multiple convictions may have to complete thirty months of treatment that includes additional conditions, such as attendance at Alcoholic Anonymous meetings. Some states may even require inpatient treatment programs for substance abuse. A DWI/DUI sentence may also include community service, such as volunteer work for charities or talking in front of school groups on behalf of an anti–drunk driving organization.

CHAPTER 5

FACING THE CONSEQUENCES

Most DWI/DUI offenders don't consider themselves criminals. They're shocked when they're involved in an impaired driving incident that results in an arrest and serious consequences. Most are genuinely remorseful for any harm they might have done. They often swear that they'll never do it again. By imposing penalties for a DWI/DUI offense, the justice system aims to help them keep that resolution.

An offender convicted of a first-time offense, however, probably has no idea of the far-reaching extent of the consequences. After the court proceedings are over and a sentence is handed down—and perhaps after time is served—a DWI/DUI conviction continues to impact an offender's life. Even if nobody was injured in the incident, the offender will be dealing with repercussions of the conviction for years. It involves the court system and the DMV, as might be expected, but a DWI/DUI can also affect auto insurance costs, job prospects, and student financial aid packages, not to mention relationships with family, friends, peers, and coworkers.

AFTER THE CONVICTION

Once an offender has been convicted of a DWI/DUI, he or she must complete the requirements of the sentence. As mentioned earlier, some of the penalties can be dealt with quickly, such as paying a fine or spending twenty-four hours in jail. Others take longer to fulfill, such as DUI education programs or reinstatement of a driver's license.

This period of restricted driving privileges is known as probation. The law allows offenders to be sentenced to a certain amount of jail time, yet the maximum is rarely imposed. It is understood that in exchange for being allowed to walk free, the offender will comply with the conditions of probation.

Probation is different from parole. Both are contingent on the promise of good behavior, but probation is granted in lieu of an incarceration during the sentencing process. Parole, by contrast, refers to the early conditional release of an offender who has already spent time in jail or prison.

Probation is a very common disposition in the juvenile justice system. The terms of the penalty allow the court to monitor a young offender's rehabilitation process. Even before the judge hands down a penalty for a DWI/DUI offense, a probation officer compiles a disposition report including relevant information such as the offender's juvenile record, personal history, and family circumstances. Afterward, the probation officer monitors the offender to ensure that he or she does not violate the terms of probation.

In criminal court, lesser offenses may be subject to informal probation, also called summary probation. The offender is not assigned a probation officer. Instead, he or she may be required to periodically report to court to

This young offender was placed under the supervision of a probation officer, who monitors him to ensure that he is complying with the conditions of probation.

provide proof of compliance with the terms of probation. In this case, failure to appear is in itself a probation violation. Other terms of probation don't require court involvement. An ignition interlock device is automated. Confirmation of completion of DUI education and any other required programs is handled administratively.

To complete the terms of probation, an offender must meet certain conditions—such as completing community service hours—and must comply with certain day-to-day limitations, such as a restricted driver's license. Other conditions may include a requirement that the offender maintain a clean criminal record during this period. Remember, for someone with a suspended driver's license, driving counts as a criminal offense. In addition, some states may impose a zero tolerance BAC requirement— any measurable BAC while driving is a violation—or may require that offenders remain substance free during drug or alcohol treatment programs.

Failure to follow through with probation terms can lead to a judge modifying or revoking probation terms and implementing more stringent penalties for the original offense. There will be separate penalties for probation violation, as well. These measures are much likelier to include time in jail or prison. The judge may even issue a warrant authorizing the police to arrest the offender.

Probation requirements for serious offenders and repeat offenders are stricter. They are more likely to be put under the supervision of a probation officer during a formal probation period.

LONG-TERM CONSEQUENCES

The impact of a DWI/DUI conviction lingers even after the successful completion of probation requirements. One of the first complications an offender might notice involves automobile insurance. DWI/DUI offenders are a bad bet for automobile insurers. Insurance companies set their rates based on risk, and people caught driving drunk represent a high risk. Insurers often cancel policies outright in the aftermath of a DWI/DUI conviction. Even if an offender is able to keep a policy, the cost of the insurance, called premiums, will double or even quadruple. These fees will eventually go down if the driver keeps a clean record, but premiums remain elevated for

As explained previously, laws surrounding DWI/DUI offenses vary greatly from one state to another. Under the Constitution, the federal government does not have the authority to impose conditions interfering with states' rights to determine their own laws. But the federal government can use unfunded mandates to pressure states to adopt certain measures. For example, in 1984, the National Minimum Drinking Age Act required states to change their own laws setting a minimum drinking age to twenty-one. States had the option of refusing, but any state that did not raise the minimum drinking age to twenty-one would have its federal funding for highways cut by 10 percent. By 1988, every state had complied with the requirements of the act. The federal government has also used this tactic to encourage states to adopt open-container laws and strengthen laws targeting repeat DWI/DUI offenders.

STATE LAWS AND FEDERAL MANDATES

at least three to five years. It can take as long as ten years for the driver to regain the preferred risk status that he or she may have had before the DWI/DUI. In addition, insurance companies may refuse to pay for any damages that occurred during an incident caused by drunk driving.

Almost all states require drivers to have auto insurance. Since insurance costs rise after a DWI/DUI, the state may require that the offender prove that he or she can afford to pay for insurance before reinstating a suspended driver's license. The insurance company sends the agency a certificate confirming that the offender

Insurance companies consider teens to be high-risk drivers, and an agent may decide that a teenager with a DWI/DUI conviction is too high risk to insure.

meets minimum insurance coverage requirements, charging a fee for the service.

Once an offender has been convicted of a DWI/DUI offense, it appears on his or her criminal or juvenile record. This information is disclosed to anyone who does a background check on the individual. Employers and landlords, for example, commonly run background checks on applicants. A criminal record can hurt someone's chances of being offered a job or a lease on an apartment. Schools also ask about criminal offenses on college applications and other forms. If disclosure is required, hiding a conviction can lead to a revocation of any offers or even a perjury charge. In some fields, such as health care, education, and law, a DWI/DUI offense can affect professional certification.

In addition to being listed on an offender's criminal or juvenile record, a DWI/DUI conviction appears on the individual's driving record maintained by the DMV. A thorough background check will probably turn up the conviction on both sets of records.

An offender who has completed probation and wants to avoid being dogged by a criminal record can apply to have his or her record sealed or expunged. In general, having a record sealed means that a court order is required to access the record. Expungement (also called expunction) means that the record is erased and the offender has a clean record once again. The laws concerning sealing and expunging records vary from one state to another. Some states permit only sealing of records. In others, the two terms are used interchangeably.

An individual acquires an arrest record even if he or she is arrested but not convicted. These records are also likely to be eligible to be sealed or expunged. A defendant who is found not guilty can immediately apply for expungement.

Expungement generally means that the offender does not have to admit to a past conviction, but there are some exceptions. Disclosure may be required in

DMV records can easily be accessed by law enforcement and, in many states, by employers, insurance companies, attorneys, and private investigators.

applying to colleges or for professional licenses. If the offender is convicted of a subsequent DWI/DUI, the expunged conviction may still count as a prior offense. In some states, an expunged record may be admitted as evidence in court if the offender is later charged with another crime.

A DWI/DUI offender must apply to the court to have a criminal record cleared, and a number of factors determine whether it is likely to be approved. A certain amount of time must elapse before the court will review an application. This may coincide with the completion of probation, or there may be a required waiting period. The severity of the offense is also a consideration. A first-time misdemeanor DWI/DUI with no aggravating factors is likely to be eligible for expungement, though a few states ban any expungement of a DWI/DUI. Records of more serious offenses may be eligible to be sealed but not expunged. Very serious crimes are generally not eligible to be sealed or expunged. Expungement is not a guaranteed process—the court may consider an offender's subsequent behavior in deciding whether to grant an expungement. If an application is denied, the offender may be required to wait a certain amount of time before reapplying.

Juvenile records are also eligible to be sealed or expunged. There's a common misconception that juvenile records are automatically sealed when an offender turns eighteen. Although some jurisdictions do automatically seal or expunge juvenile records, others require an application. The process is sometimes more straightforward than expungement of an adult criminal record, but complete expungement is not guaranteed. Some offenses cannot be expunged until a certain amount of time has passed, regardless of age. Serious offenses may not be eligible for expungement, even if they're part of a juvenile record.

Even if a criminal or juvenile record is expunged, a DWI/DUI may still appear on an offender's driving record. In some states, the DMV automatically clears a conviction after a certain period of time. In others, expungement is not possible. An offender should check his or her driving record—usually available online through the DMV—and find out if the state offers a procedure for having a DWI/DUI expunged from a driving record.

MOVING AHEAD AND GROWING UP

In early 2014, the nineteen-year-old pop star Justin Bieber was arrested for a DUI and resisting arrest in Miami, Florida. Bieber had had previous run-ins with the law, but the arrest marked his first impaired driving incident. Although he failed a field sobriety test, his BAC did not exceed the 0.02 limit. A urine test showed that he had been using marijuana and the prescription drug Xanax.

Bieber's lawyer agreed to a plea deal in which the singer pleaded guilty to the lesser charges of careless driving and resisting arrest. The sentence included anger-management classes, an educational program, and a fine. CNN reported that the judge expressed hope that Bieber would learn from the experience. "His whole life is ahead of him and he just hopefully will get the message. He will grow up."

The judge's words provide good guidance for any young person facing a DWI/DUI charge. The legal

Arrested in 2014 in Miami, Florida, pop star Justin Bieber was released on bond following an arraignment hearing. In Bieber's plea deal, he was required to have twelve hours of anger-management counseling, attend a program that teaches about the impact of drunken driving on victims, and make a large financial donation to a youth charity.

consequences of a DWI/DUI may be the most pressing concern in the aftermath, but there are also social and emotional consequences. After the initial panic subsides, a young offender may be flooded with guilt and shame. Individuals suddenly embroiled in the legal system often feel fear and helplessness at the abrupt loss of control over their own lives. Other conflicting reactions, from anger to depression, may follow. Relationships with family and friends are changed. People might

wonder how far they should put their trust in someone who made the decision to drive drunk or impaired.

Many of the penalties for a DWI/DUI focus on rehabilitation. A young offender should take DUI education and other required programs very seriously. Even if someone doesn't consider himself or herself to be an alcoholic or drug addict, the fact of the arrest demonstrates that there's a problem with alcohol or drugs in that person's life. Rather than trying to deny it, a young offender should admit the problem and take some valuable life lessons from the experience. At the same time, it's important to avoid being so hard on oneself that one feels hopeless and worthless. A young person's whole life is still ahead of him or her, as Bieber's judge said. Young adults can make a mistake, even a major mistake like a DWI/DUI, pay the price, learn from the experience, and demonstrate that they possess the resilience to get their lives back on track.

1. What are the minimum and maximum penalties for a first-time DWI/DUI offense with no aggravating circumstances in my state?

2. Does my state have zero tolerance laws for drivers under the age of twenty-one?

3. Does my state have per se laws concerning drugged driving?

4. What are some signs that a driver might be impaired, and what evidence counts as probable cause for the police to stop a driver?

5. What are the penalties for refusing to take a mandatory BAC chemical test during a DWI/DUI arrest in my state?

6. Under what circumstances can a DWI/DUI be charged as a felony rather than a misdemeanor in my state?

7. Does the law in my state allow the court to impound, immobilize, or seize a car as a DWI/DUI penalty or revoke the registration?

8. Can an underage DWI/DUI offender whose license was suspended or revoked be granted a temporary or hardship license in my town?

9. Does a DWI/DUI arrest or conviction have to be disclosed on college applications and on applications for financial aid?

10. If I have a juvenile court record, is it automatically expunged when I turn eighteen? And is a juvenile DWI/DUI conviction eligible for expungement?

AVOIDING A DWI/DUI

Drunk driving prevention measures represent the collective actions of many individuals, from the experts who shape policy to the police officers who enforce the laws to high school kids like you. If you make good, informed decisions about drugs, drinking, and driving, you can contribute to the effort by doing your part to keep yourself and your friends safe.

An Ongoing Effort

Much of the success in reducing impaired driving casualties is credited to legislation targeting drunk drivers. During the 1980s and 1990s, the legal BAC for drivers was lowered, penalties for repeat offenders were strengthened, and enforcement efforts were increased. Various government agencies continue to conduct research and promote new measures intended to combat impaired driving. In 2013, for example, the NTSB recommended that states reduce the BAC cutoff from 0.08 to 0.05. The Centers for Disease Control and Prevention (CDC) approaches drunk driving from a public health perspective. It has made recommendations such as increased use of ignition interlock devices and expanded screening for drinking problems during routine health checkups. The NHTSA studies both drunk and drugged driving and has

Relatives of victims of drunk driving crashes hold up pictures of their loved ones during a rally in Washington, D.C., that was orga nized by MADD.

recommended, for example, that states improve record systems related to drugged driving and enact laws specifically addressing drugged driving. Several agencies within the Department of Justice work to develop policies and campaigns aimed at reducing rates of drunk driving offenses.

Organizations such as MADD succeeded in the 1980s in changing public perception of drunk driving.

Some schools enact mock DUI events to raise awareness about the dangers of drunk driving. Here, an East Peoria, Illinois, senior plays a student injured in a prom-night crash.

Newfound widespread outrage over the innocent victims of drunk driving crashes and support of new restrictions helped lawmakers succeed in enacting anti–drunk driving measures. Today, groups such as MADD continue to raise awareness about the consequences of drunk driving and provide anti–drunk driving programs.

State, community, and school programs also address the issue of impaired driving. As seen, state laws concerning DWI/DUI offenses vary greatly in severity of penalties and implementation of new measures such as the ignition interlock device. One well-regarded measure aimed at adolescents is a system of graduated driver licensing

STUDENTS AGAINST DESTRUCTIVE DECISIONS

If you're interested in joining an organization dedicated to educating your peers about issues such as drunk driving, you might consider Students Against Destructive Decisions (SADD). Founded in 1981 as Students Against Driving Drunk, the organization was organized to encourage students to say no to drunk driving. Since then, its mission has expanded to include preventing other destructive decisions such as drug use, teen violence, and teen suicide. SADD is known for its Contract for Life, an agreement in which both a teen and a parent or other adult swear to avoid making destructive decisions. If your school doesn't have a SADD chapter, check out the SADD website at http://www.sadd.org to learn about organizing one.

In a SADD-sponsored "2 out of 5" campaign, some students wore caution ribbons, representing the two out of five of teens who will be involved in alcohol-related crashes in their lifetimes.

laws. A new driver must drive safely during a learner's permit and provisional license stage before being granted a full license. Drivers with only a provisional license are restricted in terms of number of passengers and night-time driving. The procedures are intended to reduce overall crashes, and they have been shown to reduce teen drunk driving, as well.

Community programs play an important role in reducing impaired driving. Examples of community actions include local open-container ordinances, law enforcement operations targeting stores that sell alcohol to minors, and ride services that keep impaired drivers off the road by giving them a ride home. Local governments also have some control over the prosecution and possible penalties for DWI/DUI cases.

Schools educate students about the risks of drunk driving. Driver's education classes, in particular, often include a section on the dangers of drinking and driving. Students learn about the physical effects of alcohol, calculate BAC levels, watch videos on the dangers of drunk driving, and try to walk a straight line wearing "drunk goggles," which simulate the visual effects of impairment. Some schools also offer events such as postprom parties at which students can have a fun, safe, drug- and alcohol-free time on an evening that's notorious for risky behavior.

Know Your Facts

It's easy to give a short answer on how to avoid a DWI/DUI: don't drink and drive. But this simple rule is easier to follow on paper than in a social situation where-everyone is having a great time and nobody is likely to think hard about the consequences of taking risks. When alcohol is involved, people who usually make good choices might start to rationalize the terrible decision to drive drunk. "I'm not too drunk to drive." "I'll drive extra carefully." "It's just a short drive." "There's not much traffic." "I have a high tolerance for alcohol." "I'll be sober enough to drive after I wait a half hour and have some coffee." These excuses don't justify drinking and driving—they just show that alcohol affects one's judgment.

Awareness about the real effects of alcohol can act as a counterpoint to the excuses that drinking and driving can be safe under some circumstances. Calculate what your BAC would be after one, two, or three drinks and review the facts about impairment—visual tracking and judgment is affected at a BAC of just 0.02. Remember that it takes a certain amount of time for alcohol to be metabolized in the body, which means that someone who is noticeably intoxicated will not be in any condition to drive anytime soon. And, if someone says, "Everybody does it—I won't get stopped or have an accident," review with him or her the statistics about teen drinking and driving. Young adults who drink and drive are at a greater risk of being in a crash than older drivers. In nearly a quarter of fatal crashes involving young adults, the driver had been drinking.

In addition, remind yourself of the consequences of a DWI/DUI conviction. Everyone knows that the penalties are harsh for an underage DWI/DUI, but specific details might serve as an extra incentive to stay away from drinking and driving. As seen, a DWI/DUI can lead to a suspended license, mandatory DUI education, heavy fines and fees, a cancelled auto insurance policy, a possible stay in juvenile detention or jail, and a juvenile or criminal record. Because of laws intended to curb underage drinking, an underage DWI/DUI can also affect a "social host" who provides alcohol to minors. In some cases, he or she may be held liable if the minor gets in a crash while driving drunk.

MAKE A PLAN

Efforts to reduce underage drunk driving have been accompanied by a wider effort to curb overall underage drinking. Strategies include targeting places that sell alcohol to minors, cracking down on big parties attended by underage drinkers, and imposing heavy taxes on alcohol. Although rates of drinking by high school students have been falling over the past two decades, a Monitoring the Future survey found that in 2013, 39 percent of twelfth graders and 26 percent of tenth graders had drunk alcohol in the past month.

Considering these statistics, it's a good idea for any teenager to have a plan prepared for situations when alcohol is available—specifically, a plan to prevent

For practice, rehearse what you would say to a friend if a situation arose in which you had to take away his or her keys to prevent that friend from driving drunk.

anyone in the crowd from driving drunk. One option is naming a designated driver ahead of time. Another is having alternate means of transportation available—you could call a cab or take public transportation, if you live in a city.

According to the CDC, in 2013, 22 percent of all teens reported having ridden with a driver who had been drinking alcohol. It's not easy to stand up to your friends and tell them that they're too impaired to drive, especially when it's inconvenient for everyone. It's even harder to prevent friends from driving drunk by insisting that they hand over their keys. But that's what you should do if you realize that someone who's too impaired to drive is getting ready to take the wheel.

As you've seen, one of the penalties for DWI/DUI offenses is attending DUI education, at which offenders receive alcohol education and sometimes counseling. A DWI/DUI can serve as a shocking wake-up call that someone has a problem with alcohol or drugs. Public health professionals urge people to get help before a drinking problem can cause damage to their health, work, or personal life. If you're concerned that a friend or family member has issues with alcohol or drugs, talk to him or her about it. If that person is willing to listen and make an effort to change his or her behavior, that could be one step toward making a difference before extreme consequences such as a DWI/DUI arrest force your friend or family member to recognize that he or she has a substance abuse problem.

GLOSSARY

analogous Describes something that has an analogy to something else; similar in some respect to something else.

blood alcohol concentration (BAC) The amount of alcohol in a person's blood, expressed as a percentage.

case A legal dispute that is heard in a court of law.

community service Work performed by offenders as part of their sentence.

convict To find someone guilty of committing a crime.

defendant Someone who has been accused of committing a crime.

disclose To make known or reveal, such as information that had been private.

disposition The final determination in a case; the juvenile justice equivalent of a court sentence.

diversion A type of informal probation in which a case is not formally processed by the juvenile court.

driving while intoxicated/driving under the influence (DWI/DUI) The offense of driving while impaired by alcohol or drugs.

expungement The act of erasing or canceling out.

felony A serious crime; specifically, a federal crime for which the punishment may be death or imprisonment for more than a year.

misdemeanor A minor crime; specifically, one punishable by a fine and by a term of imprisonment less than one year.

offender One who has committed an illegal act.

penalty A punishment imposed for breaking a rule or law.

probation The act of suspending an offender's sentence and allowing him or her to go free subject to certain conditions.

prosecutor The attorney who pursues legal action against someone in court on behalf of the government.

rehabilitation The restoration of an offender to a law-abiding individual.

sanction A penalty for breaking the law.

social history Personal and family history of a juvenile or any other person who is involved in a juvenile court proceeding, including information about the prior record of the person with the juvenile court.

status offense Conduct that is illegal for a juvenile but noncriminal for an adult.

substance abuse The use of illegal drugs or the inappropriate use of legal drugs or alcohol.

ticketable Being able to be issued with a ticket for some wrongdoing.

FOR MORE INFORMATION

AAA Foundation for Traffic Safety
607 14th Street NW, Suite 201
Washington, DC 20005
(202) 638-5944
Website: https://www.aaafoundation.org
The AAA Foundation for Traffic Safety aims to identify traffic safety problems, foster research that seeks solutions, and disseminate information and educational materials.

Canadian Centre on Drug Abuse
75 Albert Street, Suite 500
Ottawa, ON K1P 5E7
Canada
(613) 235-4048
Website: http://www.ccsa.ca
The Centre on Drug Abuse works to reduce alcohol- and drug-related harm.

DoSomething.org
19 West 21st Street, Eighth Floor
New York, NY 10010
(212) 254-2390
Website: https://www.dosomething.org
More than three million young people have become members of this organization to campaign for various causes, including working to end poverty and violence in communities.

Mothers Against Drunk Driving (MADD)

MADD National Office

511 East John Carpenter Freeway, Suite 700

Irving, TX 75062

(877) 275-6233

Website: http://www.madd.org

MADD aims to aid the victims of crimes performed by individuals driving under the influence of alcohol or drugs and to increase public awareness of the problem of drinking and drugged driving.

National Association of Criminal Defense
Lawyers (NACDL)

1660 L Street NW, 12th Floor

Washington, DC 20036

(202) 872-8600

Website: http://www.nacdl.org

The NACDL aims to ensure justice and due process for persons accused of crimes and promote the proper and fair administration of criminal justice.

National Highway Traffic Safety
Administration (NHTSA)

1200 New Jersey Avenue SE, West Building

Washington, DC 20590

(888) 327-4236

Website: http://www.nhtsa.gov

The NHTSA aims to save lives, prevent injuries, and reduce economic costs due to road traffic crashes through education, research, safety standards and enforcement activity.

National Organizations for Youth Safety (NOYS)

9401 Battle Street

Manassas, VA 20110

(571) 367-7171

Website: http://noys.org

NOYS is a coalition of organizations and government agencies working together toward the common goal of addressing health and safety issues that affect youth in the United States.

Students Against Destructive Decisions (SADD)

255 Main Street

Marlborough, MA 01752

(877) 723-3462

Website: http://www.sadd.org

SADD is a peer-to-peer education, prevention, and activism organization dedicated to preventing destructive decisions, particularly underage drinking, other drug use, risky and impaired driving, teen violence, and teen suicide.

Substance Abuse and Mental Health Services Administration (SAMHSA)

1 Choke Cherry Road

Rockville, MD 20857

(877) 726-4727

Website: http://www.samhsa.gov

SAMHSA aims to reduce the impact of substance abuse and mental illness on America's communities.

Traffic Injury Research Foundation (TIRF)
171 Nepean Street, Suite 200
Ottawa, ON K2P 0B4
Canada
(613) 238-5235
Website: http://www.tirf.ca

TIRF is the Canadian source for international research related to the human causes and effects of road crashes, providing objective and scientific information to support the development, implementation and evaluation of road safety programs, effective advocacy, and consultation.

WEBSITES

Because of the changing nature of Internet links, Rosen Publishing has developed an online list of websites related to the subject of this book. This site is updated regularly. Please use this link to access the list:

http://www.rosenlinks.com/411/DWI

FOR FURTHER READING

Gass, Justin T. *Alcohol*. New York, NY: Chelsea House Publishers, 2010.

Gravelle, Karen. *The Driving Book: Everything New Drivers Need to Know but Don't Know to Ask*. New York, NY: Walker & Company, 2015.

Greenfield, Beth. *Ten Minutes from Home: A Memoir*. New York, NY: Harmony Books, 2010.

Jacobs, Thomas A. *What Are My Rights? Q&A About Teens and the Law*. Minneapolis, MN: Free Spirit Publishing, 2011.

Jacques, Michele Siuda, ed. *Teen Driving*. Detroit, MI: Greenhaven Press, 2013.

Kane, Brigid M. *Marijuana*. New York, NY: Chelsea House Publishers, 2011.

Kiesbye, Stefan, ed. *Drunk Driving*. Detroit, MI: Greenhaven Press, 2011.

Kramer, Ann. *Teen FAQ: Drugs*. Mankato, MN: Franklin Watts, 2010.

Kuhar, Michael. *The Addicted Brain: Why We Abuse Drugs, Alcohol, and Nicotine*. Upper Saddle River, NJ: FT Press, 2011.

Magill, Elizabeth, ed. *Drug Information for Teens*, 3rd ed. Detroit, MI: Omnigraphics, 2011.

Nelson, David. *Teen Drug Abuse*. Detroit, MI: Greenhaven Press, 2010.

Netzley, Patricia D. *How Serious Is Teen Drunk and Distracted Driving?* San Diego, CA: ReferencePoint Press, 2014.

Parks, Peggy J. *Drunk Driving.* San Diego, CA: ReferencePoint Press, 2010.

Radev, Anna, ed. *I've Got This Friend Who: Advice for Teens and Their Friends on Alcohol, Drugs, Eating Disorders, Risky Behaviors, and More.* Center City, MN: Hazelden, 2007.

Rooney, Anne. *Dealing with Drugs.* Mankato, MN: Amicus, 2011.

Sadler, Katharine. *What Adults Need to Know About Kids and Substance Use: Dealing with Alcohol, Tobacco, and Other Drugs.* Minneapolis, MN: Search Institute Press, 2011.

Scherer, Lauri S., ed. *Underage Drinking.* Detroit, MI: Greenhaven Press, 2012.

Shooter, Debbie, and William Shooter. *Drugs and Alcohol 101.* Orlando, FL: Off Campus Education and Publishing Inc., 2010.

Uschan, Michael V. *Teens and Alcohol.* Detroit, MI: Lucent Books, 2012.

Voigt, Cynthia. *Izzy, Willy-Nilly.* New York, NY: Simon Pulse, 2005.

BIBLIOGRAPHY

Brown, David W. *Beat Your Ticket: Go to Court and Win*, 7th ed. Berkeley, CA: Nolo, 2013.

Compton, R., et. al. "Drug-Impaired Driving: Understanding the Problem and Ways to Reduce It: A Report to Congress." National Highway Traffic Safety Administration, December 2009.

"Crime in the United States, 2012." United States Department of Justice, Federal Bureau of Investigation, 2013. Retrieved October 17, 2014 (http://www.fbi.gov/about-us/cjis/ucr/crime-in-the-u.s/2012/crime-in-the-u.s.-2012).

Dominy, Shawn R. "FAQ—Underage DUI/OVI." 2014. Retrieved October 17, 2014 (http://www.dominylaw.com/faq-underage-drunk-driving.html).

"Drinking and Driving: A Threat to Everyone." CDC Vital Signs, October 2011. Retrieved October 17, 2014 (http://www.cdc.gov/vitalsigns/drinkinganddriving/index.html).

"DrugFacts: Drugged Driving." National Institute on Drug Abuse, October 2013. Retrieved October 17, 2014 (http://www.drugabuse.gov/publications/drugfacts/drugged-driving).

"Drugged Driving." Office of National Drug Control Policy. Retrieved October 17, 2014 (http://www.whitehouse.gov/ondcp/drugged-driving).

"DUI and DWI Laws." Nolo. Retrieved October 17, 2014 (http://dui.drivinglaws.org/topics/dui-dwi-laws).

Duke, Alan. "Justin Bieber Pleads Guilty to Careless Driving, Makes Donation in DUI Case." CNN.com, August 13, 2014. Retrieved October 17, 2014 (http://www.cnn.com/2014/08/13/showbiz/justin-bieber-miami-plea).

"DWI/DUI." Nolo. Retrieved October 17, 2014 (http://www.nolo.com/legal-encyclopedia/dui-dwi).

"Effects of Blood Alcohol Concentration (BAC)." Centers for Disease Control and Prevention, October 7, 2014. Retrieved October 17, 2014 (http://www.cdc.gov/Motorvehiclesafety/Impaired_Driving/bac.html).

Esteban-Muir, R. P. "Community-Based Impaired-Driving Programs: Local Ordinances and Other Strategies Addressing Impaired Driving." National Highway Traffic Safety Administration, September 2012.

Henning, Gregory. "Disclosing Criminal Issues in Your Application: Useful Terminology and FAQs." Ivey Consulting, November 12, 2009. Retrieved October 17, 2014 (http://www.annaivey.com/iveyfiles/2009/11/disclosing_criminal_issues_in_your_application_useful_terminology_and_faqs).

"Highway Safety Law Charts." Governors Highway Safety Association, 2013. Retrieved October 17, 2014 (http://www.ghsa.org/html/stateinfo/laws).

"Impaired Driving: Get the Facts." Centers for Disease Control and Prevention, October 7, 2014.

Retrieved October 17, 2014 (http://www.cdc
.gov/motorvehiclesafety/impaired_driving/
impaired-drv_factsheet.html).

Jacobs, Thomas A. *What Are My Rights? Q&A About
Teens and the Law*, 3rd ed. Minneapolis, MN: Free
Spirit Publishing, 2011.

Johnston, Lloyd D., et al. *Monitoring the Future:
National Results on Drug Use: 1975–2013:
Overview, Key Findings on Adolescent Drug Use.*
Institute for Social Research, The University of
Michigan, 2014. Retrieved October 17, 2014 (http://
www.monitoringthefuture.org//pubs/monographs/
mtf-overview2013.pdf).

Jolly, David N. *DWI/DUI: The History of Driving Under
the Influence.* Denver, CO: Outskirts Press, 2009.

Kuhn, Cynthia, et. al. *Buzzed: The Straight Facts About
the Most Used and Abused Drugs from Alcohol
to Ecstasy.* New York, NY: W. W. Norton &
Company, 2008.

Lerner, Barron H. *One for the Road: Drunk Driving
Since 1900.* Baltimore, MD: The Johns Hopkins
University Press, 2011.

Mayer, R. "Ignition Interlocks—Toolkit for
Policymakers, Highway Safety Professionals, and
Advocates. 2nd ed." National Highway Traffic
Safety Administration. February 2014.

Miniño, Arialdi M. "Mortality Among Teenagers Aged
12–19 Years: United States, 1999–2006." Center for
Health Statistics, 2010. Retrieved October 17, 2014
(http://www.cdc.gov/nchs/data/databriefs/db37.htm).

"New NHTSA Study Shows Motor Vehicle Crashes Have $871 Billion Economic and Societal Impact on U.S. Citizens." National Highway Traffic Safety Administration, May 28, 2014. Retrieved October 17, 2014 (http://www.nhtsa.gov/About+NHTSA/Press+Releases/2014/NHTSA-study-shows-vehicle-crashes-have-$871-billion-impact-on-U.S.-economy,-society).

"Reaching Zero: Actions to Eliminate Alcohol-Impaired Driving." National Transportation Safety Board, 2013. Retrieved October 17, 2014 (http://www.ntsb.gov/doclib/reports/2013/SR1301.pdf).

"Traffic Safety Facts, 2012 Data: Alcohol-Impaired Driving." NHTSA's National Center for Statistics and Analysis, December 2013. Retrieved October 17, 2014 (http://www-nrd.nhtsa.dot.gov/Pubs/811870.pdf).

"Traffic Safety Facts, 2012 Data: Young Drivers." NHTSA's National Center for Statistics and Analysis, April 2014. Retrieved October 17, 2014 (http://www-nrd.nhtsa.dot.gov/Pubs/812019.pdf).

"The True Cost of a DUI." Esurance, 2014. Retrieved October 17, 2014 (http://www.esurance.com/violations/true-cost-of-dui).

Truly, Traci. *Teen Rights (And Responsibilities): A Legal Guide for Teens and the Adults in Their Lives.* 2nd ed. Naperville, IL: Sphinx Publishing, 2005.

Wald, Matthew L. "States Urged to Cut Limit on Alcohol for Drivers." *New York Times*, May 14, 2013.

Washington University School of Medicine.
"Graduated Driving Laws Reduce Teen Drunk
Driving." *ScienceDaily*, June 15, 2012. Retrieved
October 17, 2014 (http://www.sciencedaily.com/
releases/2012/06/120615204737.htm).

Wisely, John, and L. L. Brasier. "Drunken-Driving
Penalties Could Depend on Your Location." *USA
Today*, July 28, 2011. Retrieved October 17,
2014 (http://usatoday30.usatoday.com/news/
nation/2011-07-28-drunken-driving-first-offense
-sentencing_n.htm).

INDEX

ABOUT THE AUTHOR

Corona Brezina is an author who has written more than a dozen books for young adults. Several of her previous works have also focused on health and legal issues concerning teens, including *Alcohol and Drug Offenses: Your Legal Rights* and *FAQ Teen Life: Frequently Asked Questions About Juvenile Detention*. She also has written *The Truth About LSD* and *Hallucinogens, Uppers: Stimulant Abuse,* and *Heroin: The Deadly Addiction*. Brezina lives in Chicago, Illinois.

PHOTO CREDITS:

Cover, p. 1 © iStockphoto.com/Vincent Shane Hansen; pp. 4–5, 30 Doug Menuez/Photodisc/Getty Images; p. 8 Michael Bradley/Getty Images; pp. 10–11 Douglas Miller/Keystone/ Hulton Archive/Getty Images; pp. 15, 17 Image Source/Getty Images; pp. 18–19 Marco Maccarini/E+/Getty Images; pp. 22–23 Stock-Asso/Shutterstock.com; pp. 24–25, 86–87 © AP Images; pp. 26–27 Photo Researchers/Science Source/Getty Images; p. 28 Colin McConnell/Toronto Star/Getty Images; pp. 38–39 Trista Weibell/E+/Getty Images; pp. 43–44 Rich Legg/Vetta/Getty Images; pp. 46–47 Scott Shapiro/Photolibrary/Getty Images; p. 49 © iStockphoto.com/photographereddie; pp. 50–51 Dave & Les Jacobs/Blend Images/Getty Images; pp. 54–55 Sean Justice/ Photonica/Getty Images; p. 58 James Porter/Photolibrary/ Getty Images; p. 61 Peter Dazeley/Photographer's Choice/ Getty Images; pp. 62–63 clearstockconcepts/E+/Getty Images; pp. 64–65 Hervé de Gueltzl/Photononstop/Getty Images; pp. 70–71 Photofusion/UIG/Getty Images; pp. 74–75 Ethan Myerson/E+/Getty Images; pp. 76–77, 88 The Boston Globe/ Getty Images; pp. 80–81 Uri Schanker/Getty Images; p. 85 Tom Williams/CQ Roll Call/Getty Images; pp. 92–93 Jon Schulte/E+/ Getty Images.

Designer: Les Kanturek; Editor: Kathy Kuhtz Campbell